Dinosaurs and Prehistoric Animals
Giant Ground Sloth

by Janet Riehecky

Consulting Editor: Gail Saunders-Smith, PhD

Consultant: Jack Horner, Curator of Paleontology
Museum of the Rockies
Bozeman, Montana

Capstone
press®

Mankato, Minnesota

Pebble Plus is published by Capstone Press,
151 Good Counsel Drive, P.O. Box 669, Mankato, Minnesota 56002.
www.capstonepress.com

1 2 3 4 5 6 14 13 12 11 10 09

Library of Congress Cataloging-in-Publication Data
Riehecky, Janet, 1953–
        Giant ground sloth / by Janet Riehecky.
        p. cm. — (Pebble Plus. Dinosaurs and prehistoric animals)
        Summary: "Simple text and illustrations present prehistoric giant ground sloths, how they
looked, and what they did" — Provided by publisher.
        Includes bibliographical references and index.
        ISBN-13: 978-1-4296-0036-1 (hardcover)
        ISBN-10: 1-4296-0036-5 (hardcover)
        1. Sloths, Fossil — Juvenile literature. 2. Megatherium — Juvenile
literature. 3. Ground sloths — Juvenile literature. I. Title.
QE882.E2R54 2009
599.3'13 — dc22   2006102209

Editorial Credits
Sarah L. Schuette and Jenny Marks, editors; Gene Bentdahl, designer; Wanda Winch,
        photo researcher

Illustration and Photo Credits
Jon Hughes, illustrator
Wikimedia/LadyofHats, Megatherium americanum, Muséum national d'Histoire naturelle, Paris

The author dedicates this book to her nephew Eric.

Note to Parents and Teachers

The Dinosaurs and Prehistoric Animals set supports national science standards
related to the evolution of life. This book describes and illustrates giant ground sloths. The
images support early readers in understanding the text. The repetition of words and phrases
helps early readers learn new words. This book also introduces early readers to subject-specific
vocabulary words, which are defined in the Glossary section. Early readers may need assistance
to read some words and to use the Table of Contents, Glossary, Read More, Internet Sites, and
Index sections of the book.

Table of Contents

giant sloth (JYE-uhnt SLAWTH)

Huge Hairy Mammals

Giant ground sloths
were huge mammals.
Thick brown hair
covered their bodies.

Giant ground sloths lived
in prehistoric times, starting
about 1.9 million years ago.
They lived in caves
in North and South America.

How Giant Sloths Looked

Giant ground sloths
looked like bears.
They had bearlike snouts.

Giant ground sloths
were as big as elephants.
They weighed
about 6,000 pounds
(2,720 kilograms).

Giant ground sloths

had sharp claws.

They curled in their claws

when they walked.

What Giant Sloths Did

Giant ground sloths
walked slowly.
They used their strong tails
for balance.

Giant ground sloths

stood up to eat.

They ate plants.

Giant ground sloths
had long tongues.
They wrapped their tongues
around leaves
to pull them down.

The End of the Giant Sloths

Giant ground sloths died out

about 8,000 years ago.

No one knows why.

Today, you can see

their fossils in museums.

Glossary

balance — to keep steady and not fall over

claw — a hard curved nail on the foot of an animal

fossil — the remains or traces of an animal or a plant, preserved as rock

mammal — a warm-blooded animal with a backbone; female mammals feed milk to their young.

muesum — a place where objects of art, history, or science are shown

prehistoric — very old; prehistoric means belonging to a time before history was written down.

snout — the long front part of an animal's head; it includes the nose, mouth, and jaws.

Read More

Goecke, Michael P. *Giant Ground Sloth.* Prehistoric Animals. Edina, Minn.: Abdo, 2003.

Goecke, Michael P. *Woolly Rhinoceros.* Prehistoric Animals. Edina, Minn.: Abdo, 2004.

Gray, Susan Heinrichs. *Megatherium.* Exploring Dinosaurs and Prehistoric Creatures. Chanhassen, Minn.: Child's World, 2005.

Internet Sites

FactHound offers a safe, fun way to find educator-approved Internet sites related to this book.

Here's what you do:

1. Visit *www.facthound.com*
2. Choose your grade level.
3. Begin your search.

This book's ID number is 9781429600361.

FactHound will fetch the best sites for you!

Index

Word Count: 132
Grade: 1
Early-Intervention Level: 18